IMAGES
of England

RAMSGATE AND ST LAWRENCE

THE SECOND SELECTION

Dame Janet Stancombe-Wills DBE. A unique ceremony occurred at Ramsgate town hall on Thursday 16 March 1922. The Freedom of the Borough of Ramsgate was bestowed on Councillor Dame Janet who was elected first freeman of the town. The Mayor, Alderman A.W. Larkin, is seen here presenting Dame Janet with a certificate of freedom of the borough, enclosed in a handsomely decorated and enamelled silver gilt casket which was designed and made by Mr P.F. Weeks, of a well-known local firm of jewellers. Dame Janet's many acts of benevolence, generosity and untiring effort for the people are well known. The portrait hanging above the Mayor is of Queen Victoria, and was painted by local artist Mr Fowler and placed in the town hall in 1840, in the presence of Princess Sophia. In the bottom left-hand corner is Mrs Dunn, another lady of eminence.

IMAGES
of England

RAMSGATE AND ST LAWRENCE

THE SECOND SELECTION

Compiled by
Don Dimond

TEMPUS

First published 2002
Copyright © Don Dimond, 2002

Tempus Publishing Limited
The Mill, Brimscombe Port,
Stroud, Gloucestershire, GL5 2QG

ISBN 0 7524 2460 2

Typesetting and origination by
Tempus Publishing Limited
Printed in Great Britain by
Midway Colour Print, Wiltshire

Acknowledgements

Many thanks to everyone who has assisted me with information and encouragement to produce this book. In particular I would like to thank the following people: John Williams, N. Hodges, Joyce Burlinson, Barrie Wootton, Davie Terry Richards, staff of the Ramsgate Library and finally Sandi Dimond, for typing the manuscript.

Sources

C.T. Richards, Fragments of History: Ramsgate
John Huddlestone, Ramsgate Street & Place Names
Kelly's Directory of the Isle of Thanet
East Kent Times
Kent Coast Times
Isle of Thanet Gazette
Thanet Advertiser & Echo
Staffordshire County Council Library and Information Centre
Pullen's Kent Argus

Contents

Introduction

This second selection of images of Ramsgate and St Lawrence once again draws on my collection of postcards and archive photographs and will complement the first volume, compiled by Barrie Wootton and me. The first part of the book takes the form of a tour round the area, commencing with St Lawrence and continuing through Nethercourt and Ramsgate town to the Royal Harbour and sands. The second half of the book recalls commercial premises, schools, social events and transport and concludes with a brief glimpse of some outlying areas, including Pegwell, Cliffsend, Manston, Minster, Monkton and Richborough.

Much of the information in the captions is derived from newspaper archives, books and other documents held at the public library, and I would like to thank the library staff for their help during my research.

Hopefully you will enjoy these reminders from the past and – who knows – more recollections may come to light through the publication of these items, helping future generations to see how our forebears lived. I welcome further information towards this aim; even a small incident remembered can be quite useful when matched up with other items which may be in our possession. Any comments you may have can be sent to Tempus Publishing who will forward them to me.

One

St Lawrence and Nethercourt

St Lawrence parish, known as Westborough in 1673/74, has seen many changes. In October 1878, the Ramsgate Improvement Act came into operation. 1,970 acres from the parish of St Lawrence were added to the district of Ramsgate together with approximately 6,000 inhabitants. The area of Ramsgate before this Act of Parliament was passed was around 308 acres. This view depicts the war memorial, erected in 1920, and Morrison & Simonson's garage. All the buildings to the left were demolished for road widening.

St Lawrence's church, *c.* 1913. It is dedicated to Laurence, a young Roman deacon who trod the fiery path of martyrdom on 10 August AD 258. The church stands on one of the highest hills in Thanet, watching over the many thousands of inhabitants of St Lawrence. Note the superb wrought-iron fencing, removed and used for munitions during the Second World War.

St Lawrence's church bells, *c.* 1911. In the year 1615, there were five bells at St Lawrence's, though they were reputedly in a sad state of repair owing to their great age. It is safe to presume that they were recast periodically as time passed. In 1808 another bell was added, making six bells, and it was not until May 1891 that a further two bells were added. During the Coronation year of King George and Queen Mary, 1911, the eight bells were serviced and rededicated in honour of that event. 1924 saw another major renovation of the bells and, to commemorate the end of the First World War, two new bells were installed which were named *Peace* and *Remembrance*. In 1997 the ten bells were once again serviced and re-hung ready to give musical pleasure to one and all.

St Lawrence High Street, *c*. 1885. On the left is a large sign advertising St Lawrence Nursery, which was owned by C. Mirams. This part of the High Street is quite spacious; to the left once stood Rochester Lodge in its own grounds and further along were Rochester Cottages. All have now been demolished and replaced with the new Ellington Infants' School and a modern parade of shops.

Newington Road in around 1925, showing a peaceful village scene at the junction with Manston Road. The building in the foreground is Rose Cottage, then occupied by Mr Albert Henry Piddock. Sadly, this cottage was demolished for road improvements. On the right is St Lawrence Elementary School for Boys, which was sold in April 1986 for £43,000. The land had planning permission for six houses, which can be seen today as you pass this way.

Highlands Poultry Farm, Manston Road, c. 1924. Ramsgate fire brigade had to visit these premises on Sunday afternoon, 13 April 1924, when several chickens met an untimely end as a result of fire. This was confined to one of the breeding pens where several sittings of chicks were being housed and tendered by the warmth provided by mechanical 'Foster Mothers'. The brigade arrived twelve minutes after the call but it was impossible to save the shed. The flames finally extinguished, the brigade returned to their station shortly before 6 p.m.

This is a scene in the lives of two local men during the First World War (April 1915). Mr Stone and his neighbour, Mr Wall, are tilling their land using two donkeys to draw the plough. As in any war, agriculture was of great importance during the First World War to help to feed the nation. This scene was witnessed by Mr A.H. Siminson of St Lawrence.

Southwood House, residence of the Weigalls for forty years from August 1880. Lady Rose Weigall was deeply involved with charity and social work. One of her treats for the local children and the elderly was an annual party held at Southwood House. Here games, swings and donkey rides took place which were followed by a superb tea, culminating in the children and the elderly receiving presents, before they all returned to their homes. Lady Rose died in 1921.

Miss Rachel Weigall, daughter of Lady Rose Weigall of Southwood House, *c.* 1920. Like her mother, Rachel's time was taken up with charitable work. During the First World War she was involved in nursing the many wounded soldiers who returned from the continent after battle.

Mr Grainger, the head gardener to Lady Rose Weigall at Southwood House, is shown here holding one of the bombs which was dropped in the grounds during an air raid on Ramsgate in May 1915. Mr Granger spent all of his working life in service to the Weigall family, starting as a youth of eighteen in 1880. Later he was promoted to coachman. He died at his home, Southwood in Queens Avenue, in March 1937.

Some of Britain's wounded of the First World War bask in the freshly cut hay of Southwood grounds, c. 1915. Lady Rose Weigall is seated fourth from the left, with her daughter Rachel on her right, clutching a small dog. On the front row in his cloth cap is Mr Grainger, the head gardener.

Nethercourt House, c. 1913. The present building dates back to about 1702, although a house of this name has been in existence since 1254. It was once the residence of Thomas Garret, colonel commanding the East Kent Yeomanry Isle of Thanet Troop. The Revd G.W. Sicklemore (1836-1880) also lived here, for some reason preferring Nethercourt House to the vicarage at St Lawrence.

A slightly later view of Nethercourt House during the First World War, when it became a hospital for the Kent VAD. Looking closely at the picture one can see soldiers looking out through the windows; also on the extreme right there is a soldier seated convalescing in the sunshine. The building had previously been used as a mansion, farm house, vicarage and civil defence centre. It was demolished in January 1957.

Ellington Park, c. 1911. Ramsgate's first park keeper, Mr Stannard, is shown here feeding the birds of Ellington Park in front of the aviary. On these occasions he was always sure of an appreciative audience.

Ellington Park shelter, c. 1925. Gilbert Home, builder of Barryholme Hollicondane at Ramsgate, erected this splendid shelter. The council purchased a private estate with an old historic mansion house in the park in 1892. Many changes have taken place since then; the demolition of the shelter is unfortunately one of them.

Ellington Park, c. 1910. The rustic ornamental bridge and miniature lake were the centre of attraction in this once beautiful and picturesque public park, which enabled visitors to enjoy the natural beauty of the trees and flowers. Over the years various fêtes, gymkhanas and open-air concerts have been held here with great success.

Ellington Park opened on 7 September 1893. These well-laid out and cared for grounds were a monument to the Victorian gardeners, highlighting the hard work which went into keeping this open space in such pristine condition. Sadly the park shelter, like some of the trees, has disappeared. The park was originally laid out by Messrs Cheal & Sons, nursery gardeners, of Crawley.

Ellington Park in the first decade of the twentieth century. It's another year and the Battle of the Flowers begins once again. This young girl is in class N and is proud to have won second prize for her exhibit named 'Faith, Hope and Charity'. The young girl's name is unknown to me but maybe someone else may know who she is. The photographer was Walter H. Barrett.

Ellington Park, c. 1910. Kent is known as the Garden of England, so it is not surprising to find such a magnificent display of natural flowers on these children's perambulators. For this section of the 'Battle of the Flowers', the winners were: First Prize – Muriel Hope, Second Prize – J.E. Thomson and Third Prize – Winnie E. Summers. The young girls' apparel blends in wonderfully with their exhibits.

Two

Ramsgate

Vale Square, *c*. 1867. This photograph of Christ Church and the windmill in the far distance was taken from a stereoscopic view. Although the church was built in 1846, further growth seems to have been sparse so far. It would be some years before the square matured and gained some form of elegance. The oldest building in the square is a thatched cottage called The Hermitage, built around 1818.

Number 54 Queen Street, 1886. These are the premises of Messrs Poole, high-class tailors for ladies and gentlemen. The business was acquired from Mr Silver in 1878. It flourished right up until 1927 when it changed hands and became Lumer's Milliner Costumier and Furrier. Today the Sense charity shop occupies the building for the National Deaf-Blind and Rubella Association.

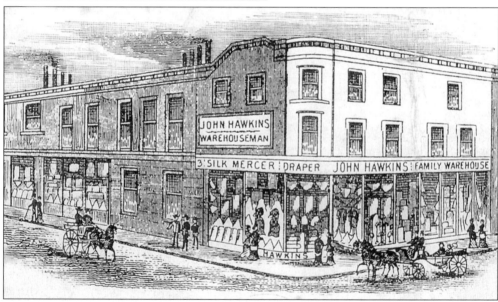

John Hawkins and family's warehouse, at Nos 11-13 Queen Street on the corner with Cavendish Street, 1886. His publicity listed his products as 'fancy drapery, silks, laces, millinery, hosiery, underclothing and haberdashery; the assortments available will be found of the most complete and fashionable nature', while 'the value offered cannot possibly be exceeded'! Such was his claim. Many years later these premises were the business of Mr Joseph Barnett, radio and electrical services. Even today the exterior has changed little.

Number 7 Effingham Place, 1865. The occupier and owner of this house and grounds was Harriet Tomson. The grounds included a field and one other house, which was occupied by a Mr John Willis. It is quite possible that the lady sitting in the garden is Harriet Tomson. The location shown in this lovely photograph is today the rear of Ramsgate fire station in Effingham Street. (Note the change in the name from Place to Street.)

Number 7 Effingham Place, 1865. This view of the grounds and garden gives one a feeling of vast open spaces. During the 135 years that have passed since this tranquil scene was recorded, we can see how, with the build-up of many more properties over the years, most of these open spaces have changed dramatically. This property, the field and the other house were rated £75. The two gentlemen seen here on the left, wearing top hats, appear to be relaxing in these natural surroundings.

Ramsgate Town Hall, superbly illuminated by the corporation gas department for the Coronation of King George V and Queen Mary, 22 June 1911. One can imagine the excitement of the townsfolk congregating at the centre of Ramsgate's civic and commercial life to commemorate this very special festive occasion.

King Street, c. 1911. This postcard was posted on 18 December to a Miss Florrie Colcreft, who lived in London. The procession is just passing the Hope and Anchor public house on the corner of Brunswick Street. The reason for this event is uncertain but it could be linked to the Coronation.

The Bull and George Hotel, c. 1905. The Bull Inn and stables in the High Street were used by the military during the Napoleonic Wars. The upper part of the High Street at this period of time was simply a lane leading to St Lawrence village, the roadway being very narrow. The hotel was destroyed by enemy bombing in 1917 and was replaced by Woolworth's and Littlewood's department stores.

Hardres Street, c. 1905. The Wesleyan church was built at a cost of £5,000 in 1810. Other sections of the street were completed during 1815. On the extreme left of the view is the East Kent Times office. On the corner of Broad Street are the premises of H. Street & Company, furnishers. In 1669 Thomas Hardres, Sergeant in Law, owned a large tract of land of which Hardres Street was part. The Wesleyan Church later became the centre of the United Reformed Church in Ramsgate. In February 1941, it was bombed by a Ju 88 aircraft; it was so badly damaged that the building had to be demolished. It was rebuilt after the cessation of hostilities.

Clarendon Gardens, *c*. 1927. The gardens were possibly named after the 4th Earl of Clarendon, Frederick Villiers (1800-1870), who was the Foreign Secretary under Palmerston, Russell and Gladstone. A butcher called Spurgeon owned this site which was aptly named Spurgeon's Field. This view from Tomson's Passage shows that little has changed in the intervening years.

Guildford Lawn, *c*. 1950. This is another area little altered by the passage of time. It was built on a site which used to be known as Brimstones Gardens and is probably named after the Earl of Guildford, who was Lord Warden of the Cinque Ports. All these properties were completed in 1842.

Cannonbury Road, c. 1903. 'X marks the place where we are staying' – not an uncommon mark to be found on postcards old and new. Ramsgate was a thriving holiday resort with numerous types of accommodation for one and all. The poster on the right is advertising animated pictures at the Palace Cinema. At the top of the road can be seen the windmill which was removed from behind Albion House to Grange Road in 1810. The sails were removed in 1900. Sadly the mill was demolished in 1937.

Southwood Road at the junction with Grange Road, c. 1927. This was a very popular area of Ramsgate, named after the wooded hamlet of Southwood which used to stand here. It has been suggested that the inhabitants used to take refuge in the woods when the Danes ravaged the coast. Today we can see that it is a very pleasant area to live in.

St Mildred's Road, *c.* 1906. Some of these properties offered bed & breakfast accommodation. The month is March, with spring just around the corner – a busy time for all landladies preparing for those families of holidaymakers who will arrive to take pleasure from our beaches, alfresco entertainers, donkey rides on the beach and many other pleasures just waiting to be discovered.

Edith Road, *c.* 1907. This view is from the junction of Napleton Road and looks towards Queen Bertha Road, only depicts a quarter of the road.

The Congregational church in Meeting Street is reputed to be the oldest religious establishment in Ramsgate. In 1662 the first incumbent was the Revd Peter Johnson MA, a former vicar of St Lawrence. The present building was erected in 1838 and Mrs James Townley, of Townley House in Chatham Street, laid the foundation stone in her eighty-sixth year. The church closed in 1978.

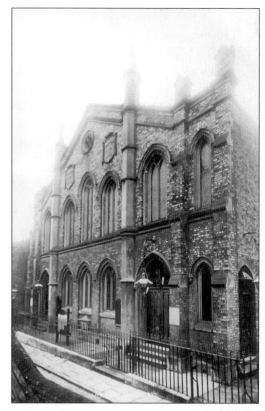

Townley Castle, c. 1917. This was originally an annexe built opposite Townley House to accommodate the Townleys' guests. The building was purchased in 1824 by Major Faussett who lived there until his death in 1832, when his niece, the wife of a Captain Glass, became the new owner. The building became a private school for a number of years, which finally at the outbreak of the First World War, when the building was used as a hospital for wounded Canadian soldiers. The building was demolished in 1920-21.

St Luke's church, *c*. 1907. The church was consecrated in 1876, though the building was not completed until 1884. The site on which it stands was presented to the parish by Mr Farley, and the Whitings donated £3,000 towards building expenses, so after a lengthy struggle St Luke's church was completed. But for the dress style of the two gentlemen in this view, one could easily believe that this is a modern photograph.

St Luke's church girls' Band of Hope, 1909. With the establishment of the church, various activities commenced. Here we have the girls all finely dressed, posing happily for this special occasion. It appears that they played tennis, judging by the racquets in the centre of the picture.

Cecilia Road, c. 1914. The inhabitants so disliked the road's original name, Cemetery Road, that it was changed to Cecilia Road. St Cecilia is the patron saint of music, whose festival is held on 22 November. This view was taken from the corner of Union Road.

Hereson Road, c. 1925. This area was once an independent hamlet, separate from the town of Ramsgate. On the right is Hobday's hardware store on the corner of Cecilia Road. This road leads on to Dumpton and the Brown Jug, an eighteenth-century inn. Also on the right-hand side of the road is Montefiore Terrace, which has changed little over the decades.

Augusta Road, c. 1913. This road is named after Lady Augusta D'ameland, who owned the Truro Estate in 1817. Lady Augusta Murray was the daughter of the 4th Earl and Countess of Dunmore. While on holiday in Rome, she met Prince Frederick Augustus, the sixth son of King George III. They married there on 4 April 1792. They had two children. Later the Duke and Lady Augusta separated for reasons unknown and the marriage was eventually declared invalid under the Royal Marriage Act of 1772.

Albion Road, c. 1920. According to archaeological records there was once a Roman encampment in this area of Ramsgate. It is not very difficult to imagine the scene during the Napoleonic era: vast open spaces and fields with rigid lines of tents, horses and guns. Times, however, change and so Mount Albion Estate was sold for development in 1865. Most of the area was bought by Mr E.W. Pugin.

Albert Road, *c.* 1920. At the peak of Ramsgate's popularity as a holiday resort, nearly every other house in the town must have catered for the people who flocked here. Royalty certainly set the example to the people and with the convenience of the railways from London and the provinces, business was to flourish. Gone are the days of the sign 'No Vacancies' which used to be placed in the front windows of many of the houses and hotels.

Thanet Road, *c.* 1913. Charles I created Sir Nicholas Tufton, Bart, the first Earl of Thanet in 1628. The earldom is now extinct. How the name Thanet originated is open to conjecture and many theories have been put forward. The one I personally prefer is derived from Lewis's *History of Thanet*. He suggests an earlier form, 'Tenet', from *tene*, a fire or beacon, which he deduced from the Celtic *tan*, meaning 'fire'. He supposes that the name is derived from the beacon fires that were maintained on high ground as warnings of invasion.

Winterstoke Gardens, *c.* 1926. The gardens were named after Lord Winterstoke and were conceived by Dame Janet Stancomb Wills. The gardens were opened to the public in 1923; they included rockeries, terraces, lawns, pool, flowerbeds and finally this elegant viewing platform and shelter. All of this fine area is at our disposal for our enjoyment, leisure and pleasure, residents and visitors alike.

Winterstoke Gardens, *c.* 1926. The gardens and shelter were landscaped and completed over a period of two years. Dame Janet Stancomb Wills paid for all of this imposing development at a cost of £10,000. The area extended as far as the East Cliff Lodge, now part of the King George VI Memorial Park.

The gatehouse and gardeners' entrance to East Cliff Lodge. This was part of the buildings and grounds bought by Sir Moses Montefiore, Bart, for the sum of £5,500 in 1831. After his death (1885) the property passed to Sebag Montefiore. It remained in the family until 1935. The last person to occupy the premises was David Nathan. Ramsgate Borough Council purchased the property in 1938. During the Second World War the Army made use of it right up to 1945, when it was returned to the borough council. The gatehouse is still in existence today and is a Grade II listed building, well worth a visit if you are passing this way.

East Cliff Lodge, c. 1817. In 1794 Benjamin Bond Hopkins purchased thirteen acres of land in Ramsgate. Here he had this splendid building erected for himself. Upon the death of Mr Hopkins the lodge was purchased by Nathaniel Jeffefys, who later sold it to James Symes, who in turn sold it to James Strange. In 1803 it was used as a summer residence for HRH the Prince of Wales. Admiral Lord George Keith purchased the lodge in 1804. Numerous famous persons stayed here, including the Duke of Wellington, King George IV and Queen Caroline. The next owner was Peter Cumming, a merchant in the Russian trade. When he died in 1832 the lodge was sold to Sir Moses Montefiore. Finally, after many more years of service, this fine-looking building was demolished in July 1953. The grounds became the King George VI Memorial Park.

The Italianate greenhouse was constructed in the grounds of East Cliff Lodge, now known as King George VI Memorial Park. Lord George Keith had it erected in 1805, mainly so that he could supply Queen Caroline, consort to George IV, with grapes whenever she stayed at the lodge. The original vine was imported from Corsica. Since the park has been in public use it is sad to see that the greenhouse has been vandalized many times. It was restored in 1981, but regrettably vandalism has taken place on several occasions since.

East Cliff, *c.* 1914. This photograph of the East Cliff shelter was taken by Beulah and Swaine, Westcliff Studio. The postcard was posted to a young lady in King Street on 24 June 1914. Unfortunately the only information I have come across are two reports in our local newspaper. One of 1904 has the headline: 'New shelter in course of construction on the cliffs' and the other, of 1913, refers to the 'East Cliff extension'. So if anyone has any information on when this shelter was built and demolished, I would very much like to hear from you.

Sherbrooke House, Wellington Crescent. Any visitor would be happy to stay here for their vacation. Ramsgate was once a garrison town and port of embarkation for the Army in the Napoleonic Wars and the military has certainly left its mark in this area, as have the visitors to Ramsgate who have experienced what the town had to offer them. Instead of military might, they can now enjoy pleasure by the bucketful: lovely beaches, varied entertainment, a wonderful coastline and plenty of fresh air.

East Cliff Promenade, c. 1910. These hotels were built on farmland which had formerly been part of the Truro Estate. The gardens, concert hall and baths built on this land in 1893 were constructed at the expense of Mr Edmund Davis, a financier who lived in St Peter's, Broadstairs. For a small charge the general public were allowed to stroll along this promenade. Today it is free to all: we may meander at will to enjoy the benefits of this fine walk.

Wellington Crescent, *c.* 1908. These elegant Georgian properties were completed in 1819; today their outward appearance has changed little. Note the weighing machine where you could try your weight for one penny. You would receive a ticket stating your weight and on the reverse side your fortune would be printed. During the Napoleonic Wars the grounds of Wellington Crescent were continually used for military purposes.

Wellington Crescent, looking towards the East Cliff promenade. At centre right is the glass-partitioned bandstand which was moved to this position in 1914. In 1825 William Miller, a local shipwright, erected a statue in oak of the Duke of Wellington. It is said that a drunken mob destroyed this effigy because they did not agree with what the Duke was doing at that time.

Madeira Walk, *c.* 1907. This is one area of Ramsgate that has not changed over the years. To see the waterfall in all its glory, with the colourful electric lighting effects, was quite an enjoyable experience. More modern transport has replaced the tramcars similar to the one seen here wending its way up the walk towards Broadstairs. This car, No. 44, was built in 1901 by Mr G.F. Milnes. On 27 March 1937 a new era commenced as motor buses took over, but as far as I am concerned the tramcar had much more character.

Harbour Parade, Ramsgate, *c.* 1932. All change here! This is a nostalgic moment for tramcar No. 52, built by the British Electric Car Company in 1903. Advertising pays judging by the number of advertisements covering this car, including the *Kent Messenger*, greyhound racing, Buchanan's Black & White whisky and Dreamland Amusements. But the advertisement I like most of all is not on the tramcar but on the side of the Popular Hotel, on the left, for Pears Soap.

West Cliff Road, *c.* 1927. This is a continuation of Queen Street, leading to Grange Road, which was once known as Sacketts Hill. Impressive private dwelling and lodging houses dominate the north and south sides of the upper area of this road. Amongst the residents were tradespeople and professionals such as dressmakers, physicians and surgeons. The pace of life seen here is very leisurely – today you would not be able to stroll down this road so casually.

A more recent view West Cliff Road. The date and photographer are unknown. These fine buildings on the south side of the road, named West Cliff Villas and Arundel, look very splendid. Today they are numbered 42, 44 and 46 respectively.

Nelson Crescent, seen here around 1929, is named after the illustrious Lord Nelson. This view shows a crescent settled into a tranquil existence. Holidaymakers who stayed in any of these guest houses and hotels must certainly have enjoyed the panoramic views overlooking the Royal Harbour. Unfortunately through the decline of the holiday trade many of these properties have been converted into flats.

Sion Hill, c. 1936. Until 1800 this area was known as South Cliff. In 1841, after a tragic accident in which a Mr Austin fell over the cliff edge, fencing was erected and later extended along Nelson Crescent and the Paragon to prevent such an accident happening again. Elizabeth Fry, the prison reformer, died in one of these houses in 1845. On the extreme left is the Foy Boat Hotel, a well-known meeting place for local people and visitors to this area.

West Cliff Parade, *c.* 1912. In 1864 this building replaced the Isabella Baths and became a boarding house which lasted well into the twentieth century. Its popularity was at its height in the 1950s when it was known as the Paragon Corner House, and was frequented by the many revellers who attended the West Cliff Hall to enjoy old time dancing.

The Paragon, Ramsgate, *c.* 1933. This part of the town was once known as St George's Fields. Most of these imposing buildings catered for the holiday trade. In the centre of this view is the Westbourne Hotel. The Royal Harbour, situated below, must have created great interest to the holidaymakers, with two fine piers and the inner basin containing various types of vessel. The visitors' favourites were the paddle steamers with their impressive power.

Three

Harbour and Sands

Coxswain Charles Fish and crew of the lifeboat *Bradford*. One of their most famous rescues was from the 1,238-ton sailing ship *Indian Chief*, which was wrecked near the Kentish Knock light vessel on 5 January 1881. There the Ramsgate lifeboat crew, under the most tempestuous weather conditions, managed to rescue eleven men. Charles Fish and his crew as well as the master and crew of the tug *Vulcan* were awarded special medals for their bravery, one gold and eleven silver, by the then Duke of Edinburgh. On 12 September 1909 Charles Fish, by then retired, was again presented with another award, the Grand Prix of the French Humanitarian Society of Calais. Local photographers John C. Twyman and Son, took this excellent photograph in around 1882.

Royal Parade and Harbour, *c.* 1900. Construction of the Royal Parade began between York Street and Addington Street in 1891 to improve access to the West Cliff of Ramsgate. To the left of this view can be seen the magnificent final result of this new road. In the Royal Harbour are a number of fishing smacks. Tied up to the quay is R78 *Pilgrim* (owner W. Perrett); to the rear is R346 *Choice* (owner H. Goodbourne); and to the right is R396 (name and owner unknown).

Royal Harbour, Stoneyard and Obelisk, 1890s. When compared with a previous photograph it can be seen that the Harbour Master's House in the vicinity of the Obelisk has been removed. During 1892 the road here was widened to improve access to the Sands railway station. The colonnade a prominent feature here, would soon be replaced by the Royal Victoria Pavilion.

The Royal Parade, this extensive view of ancient buildings is a delight to those of us who enjoy the nostalgia of the past. From left to right we have the Admiral Harvey Inn (corner of York Street) Royal Clarence Baths, Royal Hotel, Albion Hotel, National Provincial Bank and Crampton's Hotel. The greatest number of these buildings soon to be demolished (1893) for road widening improvements and access to the East Cliff.

This view of the inner harbour shows the clock house, which was built and completed in 1817. The design was by George Louch. The fish market to the left was built in 1881 and during the First World War it was used as an ammunition store. During a Zeppelin raid in 1917 it was bombed with disastrous results. Later it was rebuilt but with the decline of the fishing fleet was little used. The smack in the foreground is R8 and its owner was W.T. Watson; the crew have all lined up for this remarkable photograph recording a fabulous moment of time.

Harbour Parade, c. 1899. This exquisite view of a section of Harbour Parade and the Royal Harbour is surely a delight to behold. From left to right are the Royal Oak Hotel, Castle Hotel, Alexandra Public House, Uncle Tom's Cabin, Ferridge & Co., fishmongers, and Arthur Hall, confectioners. All are soon to be demolished for regeneration. In the foreground is a magnificent motor yacht, just one of many to have graced our Royal Harbour over the years.

The East Pier, c. 1901, is one of the main features of our famous harbour. Here can be seen two large sailing craft catering for the holiday trade, making ready to take their customers on an exciting journey to the Goodwin Sands and back. Note the small motor boats fully loaded with people. Tucked behind the two sailing craft is the motor yacht shown above. The groups of sightseers on the quayside look down with interest and fascination.

The Royal Harbour, 1912. Berthed at the quayside of the inner harbour is the Trinity House vessel *Royal Sovereign*. Her station marked the Royal Sovereign Shoal which is in the area between Beachy Head and Dungeness. There has been a light vessel there since 1875. The background of white cliffs and the Paragon make an interesting picture. The reason for her visit is unknown but one can assume it was probably for maintenance of some description.

The steam trawler *Setweather*, R96, was built at Lowestoft in 1918 and was registered at Ramsgate in 1919. The owners were W.J. Ballard and others. The vessel is seen here with steam up on her way out of Ramsgate harbour. *Setweather* has had a chequered existence. In September 1934 she was found in the inner harbour heeled over, with decks awash. During a particularly low tide the water level had fallen sharply during the night, causing the trawler to settle on to a high bank of mud. As a result she heeled over and being partly filled with water failed to refloat with the tide. Eventually she was refloated and bought by Stanley Rowden who renamed her *Tankerton Towers*. During the Second World War she participated in the Little Ships' rescue from Dunkirk. Unfortunately she was bombed and sunk off the St Govan's Light Vessel on 9 May 1941; all the crew were rescued by a Royal Air Force launch.

Ramsgate Harbour, *c.* 1910. R6, *Lizzie*, was a vessel of 29 tons built in 1899 at Galmpton, Devon. The owner was F.M. Pulman. The arrival and departure of the vessels of the fishing fleet provided scenes of never-ending entertainment and great interest to young and old alike.

Ramsgate Harbour, *c.* 1920. In a sign of the times, steam has begun to replace sail, with a steam trawler prominent in the foreground. Fishing smacks can be seen on the left and the skyline is dominated by the Royal Hotel, Admiral Harvey and Crampton's Hotel. The groups of children on the quayside are obviously being entertained by a local fisherman's vivid memories. The York tea-rooms can just be seen top left of view.

The Lighthouse and Royal Harbour, *c.* 1920. On the left is Shaw's Lighthouse, built of Cornish granite. This light replaced the previous one known as Wyatt's Lighthouse, which was first lit in 1843. In the background is a distant view of the seafront properties. Entering the harbour is R120 *Caister Castle* hopefully with a large haul of fish. This vessel was built at Great Yarmouth, Norfolk, in 1914 and the owners were Rigden of Whitstable.

The reserve lifeboat, *Elizabeth Elson*, battles through high seas in November 1963 in a search to locate the missing German coaster *Dorothea Weber*. One cannot speak too highly of the men who volunteer to perform this very highly professional and dangerous task. The Ramsgate lifeboat members past and present have one of the finest records to be proud of.

Royal Sailors' Rest, *c.* 1903. Ramsgate's role as an international port goes back to the early nineteenth century when trade between Russia and Ramsgate meant that many seamen used the dock here. On 30 April 1903 a stone-laying ceremony took place, founding the Royal Sailors' Rest in Harbour Parade. The ceremony was presided over by the port missionary, Mr W.H. Dickenson. The Rest was a temporary home offering some comfort to the sailors who used the harbour. During the First World War it was used, along with many other buildings in Ramsgate, as temporary hospitals and it was here that the first Belgian wounded were received on 10 October 1914.

Lower Harbour Parade, *c.* 1907. This is a scene full of activity with around ten horse-drawn wagonettes plying their trade here, all ready to travel to the outlying districts of Pegwell Village, Minster, Monkton and even Canterbury. Note the well-dressed people milling around, and also the spacious Pier Yard where there is not a single yellow line or motor car to be seen!

Ramsgate Regatta, 1910. The Royal Harbour has always been a source of pleasure and great interest to many people. This is the annual regatta, usually held during August. Mr Dick Lambert, a well-known competitor, is trying his luck at the greasy pole. On the quayside are thousands of spectators all enjoying this well-organized event.

Royal Ramsgate Harbour, 1913. The secretary for this year's regatta was a Mr Millis; part of his job was to raise £100, usually from the licensed trade, before the event took place. (This particular year Tomson & Wotton donated £10 10s.) The events attracted visitors by the hundred as can be seen by the number of spectators lining the quay. Various competitions were held; the one shown here is called the 'Hobley Horse'.

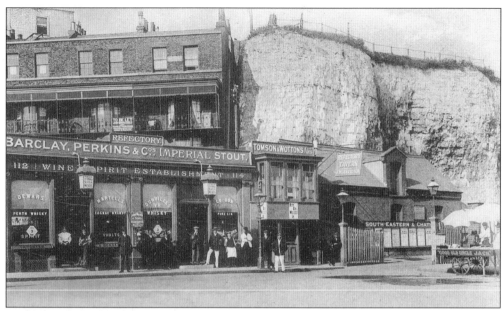

Harbour Parade, *c.* 1910. The Refectory public house was one of many Tomson & Wotton houses; it is in an idyllic position right next to the Sands railway station. The landlord, Mr J.W. Robertson no doubt looked forward to seeing many of the travellers who alighted at the station. Note there is no passenger lift to Madeira Walk in this view. In the top left-hand corner is a portion of Kent Terrace. In 1936 the Refectory was absorbed by the Harp public house.

Harbour Parade, *c.* 1911. This was an ideal position for this lift situated near the Sands railway station. It was able to carry twenty passengers at any one time to and from Madeira Walk. It was originally owned by Cliff Lifts Ltd of Falmouth Road, London. The council purchased the lift on 31 March 1919 but it was abandoned in the 1990s. As part of the regeneration programme it was reopened in 1999 and is currently in operation.

Ramsgate Sands, *c.* 1910. The ice cream stall on the left was owned by Mrs E. Tucker; her daughter states that Mrs Steed is the employee standing at the side of the stall. The sites cost between £8 and £25 each according to their position on the beach. In 1910 there were nine sites for ice cream on the sands; competition must have been very keen for the prime positions. I wonder if we shall ever see our beaches so populated in the future.

Ramsgate Harbour in November 1912. With such a practicable harbour it is not surprising that local and national sea anglers often held fishing competitions and festivals at Ramsgate. Here the Ramsgate 'D' anglers are about to board their boats with no trouble at all and in their minds no doubt are thoughts of catching something large to win the trophy and gain victory over their competitors. A note on the back of this postcard states, 'I got a prize after all, 3 large bottles of Cherry Brandy. The other person in the boat with me received a gold medal.'

King George IV arrived in Ramsgate Harbour aboard the royal yacht on 24 September 1821. He stayed with an old friend, Sir William Curtis, who lived in Cliff House, Cliff Street. The following day he continued his journey to Hanover, leaving Ramsgate Harbour to an imperial send-off by the townspeople. The King returned to Ramsgate early the following November and once more stayed with Sir William before returning to London. Some weeks later Sir William received a letter from Lord Sidmouth signifying the King's pleasure at his reception in Ramsgate and decreed that the harbour be designated 'Royal'.

The Royal Victoria Pavilion, c. 1920. It was built to the design of Mr S.D. Adshed. Princess Louise, Duchess of Argyll, opened the 'Pav', as locals call it, on 29 June 1904. Among the many famous people to appear at this venue was one Mr Alfred Sousa, the celebrated composer of marches who came all the way from the United States. Originally named Mr So, he added 'USA', his adopted country, after his name and so became Sousa! Today the Grosvenor Casino uses the Pavilion – long gone are the days of marvellous variety entertainment.

Harbour Parade, c. 1920. Ponies and carts were once a familiar attraction to be found outside the Sands railway station; it must have been very exciting for these children seated in this elegant carriage. I can recall Mr Arthur Tassam, known as the 'Cinderella Man', down by the Pavilion. Possibly this carriage could have been one of his earlier undertakings.

Harbour Parade, c. 1925. A steam engine is just visible on the turntable. The Pavilion is now advertising movies and variety. The horse-drawn carriages have gone to be replaced by charabancs and hansom cabs. The motorized age has arrived, and the changing modes of transport are well illustrated.

The Pavilion and Harbour, *c*. 1949. Though a fairly common view, this postcard has a wealth of information. At the entrance to the harbour is the twin-screw motor vessel *Royal Daffodil*, built by William Denny & Brothers Ltd of Dumbarton in 1939. The sign on the Pavilion roof is advertising Al Tabor and his band; at the lower left is a small café, where a cup of tea cost twopence; and to the extreme left is a vehicle from the Ozonic mineral water company making a delivery. The Ozonic company was a subsidiary of Tomson & Wotton Ltd.

Harbour Parade, *c*. 1952. In front of the Pier Yard is Mr Arthur Evison, who operated at this pitch with his Jockey Scales for over a quarter of a century. This popular attraction of having your weight guessed by man instead of machine was a challenge for many holidaymakers. Mr Evison was a veteran of two world wars, having served in the Royal Navy.

Ramsgate Sands, 1905. This position behind the Pavilion was a favourite for bathers and sun worshippers alike. The costumes on display here are a stark contrast to today's relatively brief two-piece costumes.

Ramsgate Sands, c. 1908. It is often difficult to date scenes from the age of greatest popularity for our beaches, as even in the late 1940s I can recall scenes very much like this though without the likes of Ellison's entertainers. Sadly this situation was to change because of the relatively cheap air fares to foreign countries, where the weather is more reliable than our own. However, today our wonderful main beach and clean bathing water still attract large crowds, especially when we have a heat wave.

Sands and harbour, *c.* 1913. Bathing machines are lined up like soldiers on parade all along the water's edge, ready for both sexes to prepare themselves for entry into the sea without any violation of their dignity. Holidaymakers to the rear are just relaxing, enjoying the sun and sands. Note the barquentine entering the harbour – just one of many interesting vessels to grace us with their presence. Today we have the Race of the Classic Ships to Amsterdam and many other events organized by the various associations within the harbour.

A common sight on the Sands near the Pier, *c.* 1913. Hordes of people often descended upon the sands amid the ice-cream vendors, minstrel shows, whelk stalls and photographers, turning this area into one giant pleasure ground. On the right is the stage for the Yachtsmen's Concert Party. Little did these people realize that their lives were soon to change forever with the arrival of the First World War.

Ramsgate Sands, *c*. 1906. For children, no seaside holiday was complete without a donkey ride on the beach. These loveable animals were sure-footed and hardy. They can walk for long periods in hot weather and difficult conditions with the minimum of food and water, making them ideally suited for beach work. The Todd family of Ramsgate worked the donkeys on the sands for over sixty years. During the summer months the donkeys were stabled in a yard at Newcastle Hill.

The Main Sands, 1914. Limited space on the beach due to the high tide did not deter the visitors who have alighted from carriages at the Sands railway station. The apparel of the ladies in this view is impressive – such wonderful dresses. Everyone appears smartly attired and well behaved, belying the rumour that the 'wrong type' of people came to our town.

The Eagle Café, situated on the end of the East Pier, c. 1939. The Grummant brothers, a firm of local builders, were contracted to build this futuristic building. Alderman W.T. Smith, Mayor of Ramsgate, officially opened the premises in July 1938. Mr E.N. Griffiths and Captain S.J. Shippick, director of the General Steam Navigation Company, first leased the building from the corporation. The café, now known as Harbour Lights, includes a dining room, sun decks and a shelter for pleasure craft customers. The total cost was £6,000. Today it is still flourishing as a popular licensed restaurant.

Merrie England, once the site of the Sands railway station, has over the years given great pleasure to untold thousands of holidaymakers and townsfolk alike. This photograph taken in the early 1950s clearly shows the popularity of our beach and amusements. At bottom left is a vehicle belonging to Holden's of Canterbury delivering soft drinks and behind it is a stall dispensing hot stewed eels at 6d, 9d, and 1s a portion. Sadly this building was destroyed by fire in May 1998.

The Sands and Merrie England, *c*. 1949. Gone are the barbed wire defences which once adorned this beach to repel invaders. This view clearly shows that normality has returned. Merrie England now displays a varied selection of amusements, food stalls, candyfloss and bingo.

Merrie England, *c*. 1950. Here is a further selection of small stalls and shops supplying the holidaymakers with entertainment and nourishment on their travels along this promenade.

Granville Marina Promenade, *c.* 1934. This is a view of the period when the Promenade was at its best. From left to right are the Marina Restaurant, some private holiday accommodation, the rifle range, the Solar Café and Dean Williams with his group of musicians.

Granville Marina Promenade, looking east with the arcade in the centre, *c.* 1934. The rifle range is advertising eight shots for 6d, just in front of the arcade is the ice cream vendor and elsewhere holidaymakers are strolling or just enjoying the sun. Over the years this complex of buildings has been used for a variety of entertainments which surely must conjure up memories from the past for a great number of people. Sadly the Marina Hall, in more recent times called Nero's Discotheque, has been demolished for improvements to our sea front. Obviously this area will never be the same again.

The Marina Parade, *c*. 1900. In the centre is the building once called The Establishment. During its lifetime it had many name changes. Sadly the Marina Hall and Pier have passed into history. Improvements have been made in this area and now as you look towards Dumpton Gap you have a fine, uninterrupted view of the cliffs. Note the brave people relaxing on the grassed area of the cliff!

Marina Sands, 1920. Ramsgate, like many other coastal resorts, attracted people who wished to benefit from the healing properties of the fresh sea air, water and sunshine, such as this lady in an invalid carriage with her companion. The picture was taken next to the Marina Hall; this site was later used for a bathing station and a magnificent pool. The benefactor for this project was the local brewery, Tomson & Wotton.

West Beach sands, c. 1938. This experimental beach was constructed with the transfer of 14,000 tons of sand from the eastern foreshore at a cost of £7,000. The first section was completed on 3 August 1935. The final cost of this project was defrayed by a legacy from the town's well-known beneficiary, Dame Janet Stancombe Wills. A.E. Moyler of 17 King Street, Ramsgate, published this postcard.

West Beach sands, c. 1960. This beach is known to locals as the 'Artificial Beach'. This was very popular with the local people and if you honoured these sands with your family you would almost certainly find a neighbour nearby. About this time there was an increase in poliomyelitis and many people blamed the condition of the sea water, which led to a decline in the popularity of this beach. In recent years the water company has improved the situation and so today we can bathe once again with confidence.

Four
Entertainers

Ramsgate Sands, 1906. This postcard was sent to a young lady, Miss Ethel Beesley, in Kentish Town. Her correspondent informs her that this postcard cost 2d; today, because of its age and rarity, it would be in the region of £5 or £6. The postcard shows Billy Breton's Pierrots standing on a raised makeshift stage performing to a large audience. There were three performances a day, at 11 a.m., 3 p.m. and 6 p.m. Seats on this occasion have been reduced to 1d each, creating a catch phrase – 'Playing for Pennies'!

Mr G. Glacco in 1907. The famous fasting man was born in 1866. His father was a major in the Austrian army. This unusual form of entertainment took place at the Royal Victoria Pavilion, where a small house was constructed by Mr Charles Collins of York Street. It was glass-fronted so that people could see him during his fast. This lasted for thirty-eight days, during which Mr Glacco lost a total of 42lb in weight.

Ramsgate Sands, September 1905. The alfresco group, seen here entertaining their audience on the sands, is unknown. On the makeshift stage are two young girls taking part in some small drama or talent competition, while the audience partake of the fresh air, open skies and the skills of the musicians and actors – all for a penny or two.

Palace Theatre, 1905. This is the final curtain after a grand performance of *HMS Pinafore* by the members of the Ramsgate Operatic Society. What a wonderful line-up of local talent and breath-taking costumes! The photographer was L.G. Carpenter.

Miss Elaine Darcia, the famous lady conductor with her band of twenty picked musicians, on the West Cliff Promenade, 11 September 1911. They played three times daily during their one-week contract. They became very popular with the visitors and residents alike and frequented the town until 1914.

Ryder's Smart Entertainers, 1914. For this year, Mr Ryder Davis secured one of the most prominent pitches on the sands, opposite the Sands railway station. They were just one group out of hundreds of alfresco entertainers who over the years have brought laughter and joy to thousands of family holidaymakers.

Mr Roxburgh Reeley's concert party, the Comedies, c. 1913-14. The venue for the concerts is unknown, so if anyone can enlighten me, I would appreciate it. One thing that stands out in this photograph is the very exquisite dress style of the ladies. I cannot imagine that this superbly dressed group would be in the open air, but I may be wrong.

West Cliff Theatre, *c.* 1936. This was the venue for Billy Merrin's Commanders, a band which had great success at Ramsgate for nearly two decades. His lead singer was Rita Williams, who later sang with the Billy Cotton Band. Billy Merrin also played with the famous Vera Lynn and Gracie Fields and the band even recorded for Decca. Sadly after the Second World War styles changed dramatically; Billy's last engagement was in Australia in the 1960s. He died in 1980 but his music still lives on.

Two local entertainers, Miss Elsie Smith and Miss Maude Milgate, displayed their talent at many concert parties during the 1940s and the 1950s. This venue is thought to be Holy Trinity parish hall. Miss Blanche Millgate, Maude's sister, was the organist at Holy Trinity church for a number of years. Elsie died on 7 September 2000 aged eighty-seven.

The Checkers Dance Band, an amateur concert party, entertain the armed forces for free under the supervision of Mr E. Butcher in the Coronation ballroom, 1940. The complementary instrumental music of the Checkers was very well known at the time. Those taking part were: Mr E. Butcher, Lucy Smith, Sidney State, Marjorie Coulson, Joe Young, H. Chapman, Alan Young, Elaine Coulson, A. Wood, Chris Berry, Wilfred Callow and Ted Jones.

The Holiday Express stage one of their many programmes of entertainment with a scintillating cast of over forty top-line artists at the Royal Victoria Pavilion, 1960. Third and fourth from the right are Billy Grant and Elsie Dunn, two wonderful dancers. Stalls seats were 3s or 4s and were worth every penny for this first-class family entertainment.

Five

Schools

A charming picture of a stage production arranged by the teachers and pupils of the St Lawrence National School for Girls, 1910. Among this large group is a girl called Ethel Read, daughter of Alice and George Read, who sent this wonderful postcard to their mother who lived at Sheldwich Lees, near Faversham. By its looks the show appears to have an oriental flavour. This fine old flint-built school building has now gone the way of many other such buildings and has been replaced by a more modern school. Hopefully this tradition of artistic performance will continue to flourish with the current pupils.

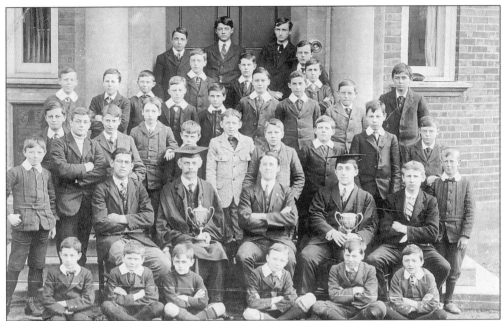

Ramsgate County School, for boys and girls, opened on 14 October 1909. Here the first headmaster, Mr H.C. Norman (of the boy's section), is seated among his pupils in Clarendon Gardens in 1911. He is holding one of the two trophies awarded for sporting or academic achievement. The original school was built to accommodate up to 170 boys and the same number of girls, both sections working independently of each other. The building costs amounted to £11,300. Today we know this building as Clarendon House Grammar School.

Clarendon Gardens, c. 1921. This is a more laid-back image of the main entrance to the Ramsgate County School for boys and girls. The ten years since the previous photograph have seen a dramatic increase in the number of pupils. This grand gathering may have been a final photo-call for the school record before the whole boys' section moved into their new premises in Chatham Street.

Chatham House School, *c.* 1916. This aerial view of the school and surrounding district once belonged to a soldier who was a patient here during the First World War, when the premises were used as a hospital for wounded Canadian troops. The school was bombed at Easter 1915 and again on 22 August 1917. This necessitated the removal of patients to a safer environment. A regiment of Highland Light Infantry replaced the Canadians. In 1918 the school became a prisoner of war internment camp and finally, after the cessation of hostilities, it was used as a Royal Army Medical Corps warehouse until 1920.

Cricket at Clarendon House Grammar School, 1924-25. The school's eleven, dressed in bright green blouses, mauve ties and navy blue skirts, pose to record their victory on the sports field. The lady in the centre is the headmistress, Miss Merryman, whose talents also included singing and dancing.

St Lawrence College, *c.* 1915. This is another large building that was occupied by Canadian soldiers for their convalescence during the First World War. Part of a message on the reverse of this postcard states: 'Tell mother my foot is still bothering me. It doesn't seem to heal up very fast. I hope it will be Canada for me soon.' This is from one of the survivors; sadly many millions of servicemen did not return, so this soldier was one of the lucky ones to be convalescing here at St Lawrence College. Today the exterior of this section of the College appears very much the same from College Road.

St Lawrence College, *c.* 1912. Swimming baths are an asset to any school! During the First World War, when the college was in use as a hospital, the bath was drained of water, a false floor was constructed and the area was used as a gymnasium, with all kinds of new equipment. There were rope ladders, bars and devices for restoring the use of damaged limbs, a great asset to the invalid servicemen. After hostilities ceased the baths were returned to their normal use.

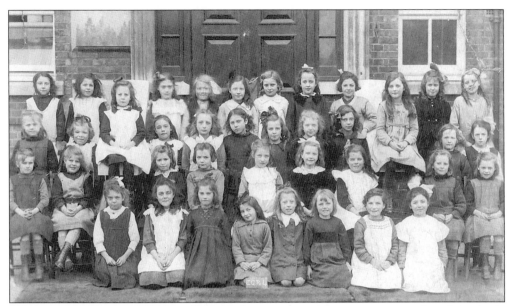

Ellington School, class EGR4, *c.* 1918. Only one name is known to me in this photograph: Ethel Florence Goldsmith, fourth from the right on the second row from the front. During the First World War, her father served in the Royal Navy aboard HMS *Verdun.* Ethel had five brothers, four of whom followed in their father's footsteps, while the fifth joined the Royal Marines.

St George's Commercial School, Church Road, *c.* 1923. These pupils are from class seven; in the centre row, fifth from the left, is Miss H.M. Smith, daughter of Captain and Mrs W.T. Smith. Captain Smith was Mayor of Ramsgate in 1937-38. Miss Smith became a teacher at Hereson Infants' School and was employed there for thirteen years. Eventually she married Mr M. Sparks, a landscape gardener and nurseryman, of Newington Road.

St Lawrence Elementary School for Boys and Girls, Newington Road, c. 1943. In June 1940 the St Lawrence pupils were evacuated. Billets were found in Marchington, Draycott and Basford near Leek, Staffordshire. Here they were absorbed into the local families and schools. Many sad and pleasant tales can be told of this period of change. As the war progressed in our favour, families became more confident and wished their children to return home, so the local need for teachers rose again. A master was recalled to Ramsgate in March 1942 to set up a temporary school at St Lawrence.

Ellington County Modern School, 1948. Judging by the happy faces of these girls, this could be their final gathering before stepping out into the world of work. The teacher in the centre is Miss Phillips. Two of the girls' names are known – Doris Debling and Ann Veasey.

Six
Commercial Premises

Woodman Inn, c. 1898. The landlord was Mr Henry Thomas Curling. This is a Cannon Brewery house, as can be seen from the sign, and the premises was to be found on the East side of Hardres Street, at the junction with Staffordshire Street. Here also was the meeting place for members of the Ancient Order of Druids (St Aethelbryht Lodge, number 425). Note the sign on the gas lamp, extreme left. Today the Burlesque Hair Stylist occupies this site. The façade of the inn has been altered little. The entrance to the inn on the right has been blocked up and access to the hair salon is by a doorway on the left-hand corner of the premises.

Mitchell's Confectioneries shop in the High Street, on the corner of Turner Street and opposite Woolworth's store, 1915. A German Zeppelin inflicted severe damage on these premises during a raid on 17 May 1915. Pinned to Mitchell's front door is a poster related to the war effort: 'Recruits wanted for the Army Medical Corps'. Today these premises are occupied by Gilham Butchers Ltd.

William Berry & Son, greengrocers at 177 King Street, on the corner of Victoria Road. During the First World War Mr Berry, along with Mrs Caroline Debling of King Street and Mr William Daisy of Packers Lane, were charged with overcharging their customers for potatoes. The borough Justices found them guilty and fined them a total of £55. The maximum price of potatoes at this time was $1\frac{3}{4}$d per pound.

F.W. Hammond, 171 King Street. *c.* 1925. This is an inconspicuous little shop but one with an interesting history. It is believed to date back to 1898. The gentleman standing in the doorway is probably Mr Hammond himself, proudly displaying on his chest a row of medal ribbons; this suggests that served in the military during the First World War. After 1948 the business changed hands on five occasions, eventually in 1974 becoming Dorman Confectioners. Today, although the flints have been rendered over, the remaining shop windows appear very much the same. Instead of confectionery it now sells antique and second-hand furniture. The shop is now called 'Just Kidding'.

King Street, *c.* 1930. William Ernst Packer's bakery shop flourished for many years and it was not until the 1930s that it changed ownership and became Cowell's Bakery which continued until 1939. The Second World War saw the decline of many businesses in Ramsgate, as once again we were in a front-line danger zone. The shop façade has now gone and the property has been converted into a dwelling house.

John Leonard Collins, late of Cole & Company ironmongers, *c.* 1925. Collins' shop, situated in York Street opposite Tesco, continued in business until the start of the Second World War. After the evacuation of large numbers of residents from the town the business was not viable and had to close along with many others. After the end of the war town life gradually returned to normal, but this once flourishing concern was lost forever. The building now houses a completely different type of business, the Cyprus Restaurant. Today, after many years of dereliction, regeneration has begun on this side of York Street.

Ainslie Brothers butchers, *c.* 1898, with a fine display of well-dressed carcasses outside. Ainslie's had two premises in the town, one at 27 High Street, just past Turner Street, and one at 88 King Street on the corner of Belmont Street. The business flourished between 1897 and 1904. The Ainslie brothers served many hundreds of Ramsgate families, including lords, ladies and royalty.

The Alexander Inn, Harbour Parade, from the Pier Yard, *c.* 1903. In 1857 an older establishment called the Dukes Head stood on this site. From 1907 the properties including the Alexandra and those to the right of it were gradually demolished for road widening, making easier access to the Sands railway station. Note the barrow and the fishermen selling their catch. Originally this postcard was purchased from J. Pain, Newsagents, at 55 High Street.

Northwood post office, 6 Highfield Villas, Newington Road, *c.* 1906. The sub-postmaster, Mr George Richards, is the gentleman on the right. The young man standing by his side is his son, Mr Bertram Terry Richards. Most people of this area will have known this former post office as the Candy Box confectioners. Today it is a private house.

Alfred Thomas Mummery, baker, 2 George Street, *c.* 1903. The previous owner of this bakery was Mr Charles Goodwin. It continued as a bakery until 1966. The 'Cook and Confectioner' sign always caught my eye when I passed along this street; being brass, it was always kept highly polished, and one could not help but to be attracted to it. When the shop closed the sign was left intact, until one day it disappeared. The Ramsgate Insurance Company was one of several businesses to occupy the premises afterwards; the current tenants are Southern Design Services.

Chatham Street, *c.* 1926. The Railway Tavern was situated on the corner of Shah Place. The Tomson and Wotton brewery owned this public house, along with many others in the town. In 1961 the name of this public house changed to the Rocket. Unfortunately it did not prosper and the brewery closed the tavern in 1970.

78

The Elms Hotel, Richmond Road, *c.* 1908. The street name seems to be derived from the Duke of Richmond, Henry Fitzroy, who was Warden of the Cinque Ports in the sixteenth century. The Elms Hotel offered good accommodation at moderate charges; bed and breakfast was 3s 6d per night. This building is still here today, very little altered. The pillared entrance has gone but it is still used as a public house.

Good accommodation, moderate charges. Bed & Breakfast ⁿ/ₐ inclusive.

Blinko & Sons, once a very well-known stationer, Queen Street, *c.* 1935. In the window is a display of photographs of King George V and Queen Mary. The bunting displayed above the shop signifies a celebration of some kind, so could this view have been taken during the Silver Jubilee celebrations for the King and Queen? In 1963, Blinko & Sons became Geering's Thanet Ltd and today the premises are occupied by Homebasics.

John Hawkings, on the corner of Queen Street and Cavendish Street, 1910. This postcard was sent as an advertisement to a customer in Broadstairs; it reads: 'Our business is increasing because our goods are reliable, our prices are right. Please visit our sale now proceeding and judge for yourself'. Today, Barclays Bank occupies the site.

Victoria Road, c. 1960. The owners of The Lawn guesthouse, like many others who owned large properties with extensive grounds, found that they were uneconomical to maintain. With the demand for new housing for the ever-growing population of the town, it is not surprising that this building was demolished so that the area could support more people. Now as you travel along Victoria Road, you will see immaculate private apartments enhancing this area of Ramsgate, still called The Lawn.

Camden Arms, 1930s. Dating back to the 1840s, this fine building can still be seen today and is still well maintained. It commands a prominent position in La Belle Alliance Square, providing food, drink and lodgings to all who may enter its premises. Once a Tomson & Wotton house, today it is a very popular free house.

The Foy Boat Hotel, on the corner of Adelaide Gardens and Sion Hill, c. 1906. In the early eighteenth century there was a watch house on this prominent site overlooking the historic Royal Harbour. At the top of the photograph there is a peculiar pennant, which was probably used as an identification point. In the evening of Sunday 7 September 1941, an air raid occurred over the town. Six bombs were dropped from enemy aircraft in this area, one of which scored a direct hit on the hotel. During post-war rebuilding a new Foy Boat Hotel was built on this site.

J.R. Parker, ironmongers, on the corner of York Street and Queen Street, *c.* 1965. The window display indicates the last few days of the closing down sale. This once very popular business gave excellent service to its many customers. You name it, Mr Parker would find it for you – nothing was too much trouble for him. The adjoining premises to the right belonged to Mr J.E. Bridges. The baker's shop, along with other buildings, was soon to be demolished to make way for the building of the Argyle Centre. The new buildings never seem to have the same charisma as the old.

Herbert Foster, sail maker, in York Street, 1961. This shop was a favourite haunt of many youths keen on river and sea angling. Mr Foster, a unique character the likes of whom are seldom seen today, would take the time to instruct you as to the best and most appropriate type of tackle to use. He is sadly missed. On the left of the shop is George Fennell's dining room and to the right, A.B. West's accountant and turf commission agents.

The shop front of Mr Peter Milgate, who supplied general grocery, provisions and confectionery, Bellevue Road, c. 1939. In its long history this shop has been a butcher's, fishmonger's and newsagent's. The daughters of Mr Milgate continued in their father's footsteps, but with the changing style of modern shopping this shop was soon converted into a private dwelling. On the right is the shop of Vye & Sons, the scene of a tramcar accident on 27 May 1905.

Bellevue Road, c. 1953. Misses Blanche and Maude Milgate stand in the entrance to their shop, 17 Bellevue Road Ramsgate, which is reputed to be the oldest shop in the road, dating back as far as 1821. These two ladies contributed much with their commercial and musical skills to the town and to Trinity church, and are fondly remembered.

Homestead Stores, Bellevue Road, *c.* 1950. The proprietors were G. Moses & Sons, the descendants of a well-known Ramsgate shipbuilding family (Beeching Moses). With the decline of shipbuilding and the fishing industry, they turned to a different type of business, which lasted until the 1970s. After Moses this shop was occupied by Austen's furniture dealers, and today we see something completely different as we pass along this road – it is now the Mother Goose nursery school.

Ramsgate Information Bureau, a section of the borough publicity department, 24 King Street, 1952. The young ladies posing for this photograph are Elizabeth Goldsmith and Doris Board. Ramsgate as a seaside town had plenty to offer our visitors: the Festival of Lights, Frederick Hargraves' dance band, Eagle steamers to Southend and the *News of the World* angling tournament were just a few of the entertainments to be offered. In recent years the town has had to compete with holidays abroad. The hovercraft and ferries have gone, but with the newly completed road to the Royal Harbour, we can perhaps look forward to a prosperous future for the town.

Seven

Social Events

Mercy Elizabeth Clara Hammon in the uniform of the Queen Alexandra Royal Army Nursing Corps, raising money for Alexandra Rose Day in 1921. Queen Alexandra (1844-1925) was consort of Edward VII. Sadly Mercy died on 2 April 2000. My kindest regards to Mr N. Hodges for this marvellous photograph.

On 13 August 1905 the Musique Municipale et des Sapeurs Pompiers de la Ville de Calais visited Ramsgate. Here the Calais band is leaving the Ramsgate Pavilion for a drive round the Isle of Thanet. Three brakes were required to accommodate the party and they travelled through Broadstairs and Kingsgate, savouring the beauty of our island. The dignitaries on board were Mayor C.R. Dowling, Mr Robert Stacey, Mr F. Smith, Mr H.J. West (former Belgian consul to Ramsgate), Mr L. Phenix (deputy town clerk) and Mr T. Kingston (town sergeant).

The declaration of the poll in the by-election held between Mr Esmond Harmsworth (Conservative) and Captain W.J. West (Liberal), at the Town Hall in 1919. Mr Harmsworth won by a majority of 2,653 votes to become the youngest member of the House of Commons. He served as MP for the constituency of Thanet for ten years.

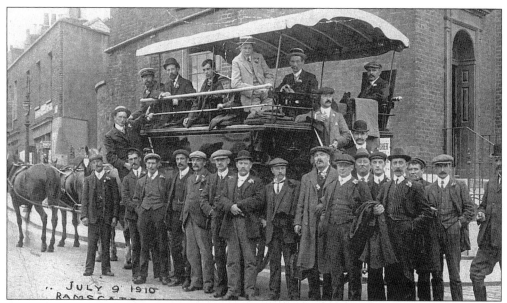

Chatham Street, 1910. Members of Ramsgate Liberal Club prepare for an unknown excursion. There are twenty-six people including the driver, so it is no wonder there are four horses to draw the brake! Second from the left on the top row is Mr T.H. Prestage, who won a seat on the borough council in 1909 and became Mayor of Ramsgate in 1928. His work to improve services, health and housing endeared him to the people of Ramsgate and he was affectionately known as 'Old Tom'.

Cavendish Street, c. 1925. These people were collecting money for the Old People's Dinner Fund. To combat widespread poverty in the days before the Welfare State, there were many such appeals; other examples are jersey and toy appeals, and funds for children and soup kitchens. Better-off members of the community often saw it as their duty to help the underprivileged by organizing events of this kind. Second and third from the left are Mrs Bussey and Mrs Harvey, while at the right-hand end are Mr and Mrs Hammond. The dinners were held in the Westcliff Concert Hall.

High Street at the corner of Queen Street, 1914. The Army displays its marching skills by parading through the streets of Ramsgate just before the outbreak of the First World War. The message on the back of this postcard states 'Just a card to let you know that it will break soon' (presumably referring to the war). On the left are the premises of Lewis and Weeks, jewellers; this building was demolished to make way for the new Lloyds Bank in 1927.

The Royal East Kent Mounted Rifles parading past the Town Hall from Queen Street, 1914. On the left are the Market, Page & Sons wine merchants and, on the corner of York Street, Parkers the ironmongers. The parading soldiers and the few spectators seem to be in a sombre mood. Soon the town would experience a new type of military event: aerial bombing by Zeppelins.

High Street, Ramsgate. The Kent Cyclists territorial force are all lined up, ready to move off to their camp at Callis Court Road, Broadstairs, after attending church parade at St George's Church, Ramsgate. There were 447 men at the camp, which was held in July 1914. The local soldiers were of G Company and their Quartermaster Sergeant was W.T. Smith, who became Mayor of Ramsgate in 1937.

Soldiers of the Kent Cyclists Battalion marching past the Town Hall, again in 1914. The recruiting area for G Company was Ramsgate, Broadstairs, Margate, Sandwich, Deal and Eastry. Battalion buglers were recruited from the ranks of the Ramsgate Church Lads' Brigade. When war was declared on 4 August 1914, the battalion was moved to Canterbury, to become involved in coastal defence duties.

A fancy dress ball on skates in Kent's largest skating rink at Dumpton Park Drive, 1911. These merry people are taking advantage of these facilities one year after the rink opened. Skating sessions were held on weekday mornings and evenings, admission 1s; Saturday mornings, 6d; and Saturday afternoons and evenings, 1s.

Early on Sunday 23 June 1914, PC Ashdown was patrolling Addington Street and saw flames issuing from the shop at 41 Albert Street. He tried to arouse the occupants at the front door but to no avail, as they lived in the rear of the premises. With the assistance of a neighbour, Mr Fred Solly, they went to the back to make an entry. A nailed-up six-foot gate barred their way, but with the help of PC Ashdown, Mr Solly climbed over the gate and found a step ladder which he used to enter through the bedroom window. Here he found Mr and Mrs Arnett and their invalid son partially overcome with smoke and fumes. Mr Fred Solly lowered the occupants from the window to the waiting arms of PC Ashdown. When Captain West and the fire crew arrived they found the building in flames from top to bottom with the interior completely burnt out. After approximately half an hour the brigade had the fire under control.

The grand opening of the new Drill Hall on Willsons Road, 23 May 1912. The band and troops of A Company, 4th Battalion of the Buffs, and G Company Kent Cyclists Battalion parade smartly and form a guard of honour for the dignitaries present. To the left is Vale Road. Willsons Road was named after a Mr Willson who lived in Dudley House, Grange Road, which later became the Savoy Hotel.

The new Drill Hall, Willsons Road, 1912. Among the dignitaries seen here are Major-General Townsend, General Sir Charles Warren, Lord Sackvill and Mr Norman Craig KC MP, all awaiting the arrival of the Mayor of Ramsgate, Charles John Gwyn. The photographer for this occasion was M. Short of 13 High Street and Royal Pavilion Studios.

The Mayor's Sunday Parade, 1913. A large procession consisting of local organizations accompanied by the mayor and corporation officials marched to St George's church. After the church service, the procession paraded back to the Town Hall and the various groups, including the Kent Ambulance Brigade, were inspected by the mayor and officials of the borough. The premises in the background are White and Ellis, drapers, on Harbour Street.

The photographic section of the 1st Gordon BP Boy Scouts on the Marina in 1913. These Boy Scouts are on a camping trip to Ramsgate but where they are from is a little mystifying. There was an organization called the Gordon Boys' Orphanage, which had establishments in Croydon and Dover, so it is possible they are from one of these. The small plaque on the table advertises photographs while you wait for 3d, 4d and 6d – certainly a fine way to raise funds.

Open-air drills of the Ramsgate Volunteer Training Corps on the Warre Recreation Ground, April 1915. Mr Warre presented this ground to the town in March 1897 to commemorate the Diamond Jubilee of Queen Victoria. On the far left is Captain Mathews and next to him is Thomas Horne. The photograph is by Ethel M. Weeks, for Simonson's of St Lawrence.

A funeral cortège for air-raid victims, St Luke's Avenue, 1916. On Sunday 19 March two enemy sea-planes dropped bombs in the neighbourhood of St Luke's. The victims included five small children, Frank Hardwick, Herbert Gibbons, Ernest Robert Philpott, and James and Gladys Saxby, aged between four and twelve. The little victims were laid to rest at St Luke's and St Lawrence's cemeteries. Following this sad event a small red and white flag was issued with 'In memoriam' on one side and 'A memorial to Ramsgate little ones' on the other.

East Kent District L Officers of the International Order of Good Templars, 1932-33. This was an organization fighting the social problems of the time, particularly poverty and drink. The order was instituted in 1890 and they met at the Forrester's Hall in Meeting Street. From left to right, back row: Mr Fairy, Mr Jorden, Mr Scott, Mr Hunt, Mr Jeffrey, Mr Impett, -?-, Mr Harvey. Front row: Mr B Susans, Miss Hawkes, Mr Knight, -?-, Mr Jacobsen, Mrs Hunt.

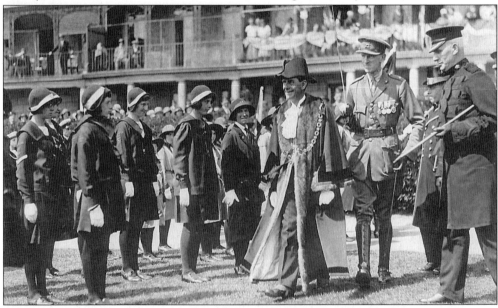

Wellington Crescent, 1935. Mayor Alderman E.E. Dye, Major C.S.F. Witts TD, 4th Battalion Buffs TA, and Chief Constable Samuel Flower Butler cheerfully inspect the young ladies of the St John Ambulance Brigade during the celebrations for George V's Silver Jubilee. Many organizations were on parade for this special occasion. Later 5,000 children congregated in Ellington Park, to be addressed by the chairman of the Education Committee. After numerous entertainments the infants were presented with jubilee mugs and the seniors with jubilee beakers.

Ramsgate National Kitchen, 1920s or '30s. During this period unemployment was very high; I can recall my grandfather arriving home late in the evening after cycling 20 or 30 miles a day looking for work. As a result, soup kitchens sprang up in many towns to feed the hungry families. In Ramsgate a small building behind St George's Hall was used.

This fine group of smiling ladies participated in the Church Army's fifteenth Summer Crusade, which started in Lichfield, Staffordshire, on 9 June 1934. Various events took place including services in the cathedral, a civic welcome and a silver band concert with community singing on the recreation ground. The Church Army's founder and leader, Prebendary Carlile, was present, aged eighty-eight. After the weekend, the ladies began their mission to thirteen seaside towns. It is not known when they arrived in Ramsgate.

St Lawrence Cliffs, 1934. Mayor and Mayoress Alderman and Mrs E.E. Dye sit proudly in a 1903 Wolseley vehicle during the fourth concours d'élégance which was held in Ramsgate on Saturday 21 July. Mr Riley, head of the famous motor manufacturing company, distributed prizes at this ever-popular motor car event.

Ramsgate Harbour, 1934. This ceremony, attended by the Mayor, took place outside the clockhouse on 1 October and marked the handover of the harbour to the Harbour Board by the Ministry of Transport.

Concours d'élégance on the Royal Esplanade, 9 July 1938. These magnficent vehicles gave great pleasure to owners and spectators alike. The competition was an annual event which attracted a vast amount of interest from residents and holiday visitors, providing an added bonus for the holiday trade.

Miss Jean Batten, the famous aviator, presents an award to the winner of one of the sections competing in the 1938 Concours d'élégance on the Royal Esplanade. After completing the awards, Miss Batten attended a gala dinner and cabaret at the Granville Hotel, part of a non-stop round of banquets, balls and receptions in her honour. With the advent of the Second World War, Jean Batten's name became less famous and she died in obscurity in Palma, Majorca, in 1982.

Reverend Harcourt Samuel OBE as Mayor of Ramsgate. His first ministry was in Lambourne End, Sussex; eight years later he transferred to the Cavendish Baptist church in Ramsgate. He became a stalwart figure in local affairs; in 1937 he was co-opted as a member of the Ramsgate education committee. In 1941 he was elected to the town council for the East Central ward and in 1942 he became chairman of the Civil Defence Committee. He took great interest in the Ramsgate General Hospital. Above he is depicted in his Mayoral Robes. He first became Mayor in 1944 and served again in 1955, 1956 and 1957. He received his OBE in 1960 and died on 3 May 1996.

Mayor Alderman Percy Turner leads a parade on an unknown occasion in Queen Street, 1951. In 1961 he was honoured with the Freedom of the Borough of Ramsgate, following twenty-six years' service as a member of the borough council, Alderman and Mayor.

West Cliff Road, 19 May 1948. On this day, Princess Marina, Duchess of Kent, visited Ramsgate to open the new landing stage at the end of the east pier and to lay the foundation stone of the new outpatients' department of Ramsgate General Hospital. Here she is seen inspecting nurses of the St John Ambulance Brigade and stopping to converse with Mrs Grace Simmon, a Sunday school teacher at St Luke's church. Accompanying the Duchess is the Mayor of Ramsgate, Alderman J. J. White and standing behind him is the Macebearer, Mr Porter.

HRH Princess Margaret at the opening ceremony of the new Ramsgate Hospital outpatients' department, Thursday 1 June 1950. She also inspected the ladies of the St John Ambulance Brigade. With her in the above photograph are the Mayor of Ramsgate, Alderman Percy Turner, and Revd Harcourt Samuel, chairman of the Isle of Thanet Hospital Management Committee.

Ramsgate Harbour, 29 July 1949. After an initial visit to Broadstairs, this group of tough and rugged invaders, very much like their Saxon forefathers, landed here in the Royal Harbour from the Danish ship *Hugin*. Here they were met by a tumultuous welcome from a vast crowd of people who were lining the quayside.

The re-enactment in July 1949 of the arrival of the Saxons Hengist and Horsa in the fifth century, their meeting with King Vortigern and his betrothal to Hengist's daughter, Rowena. It was staged by the Ramsgate Arts Society, with many other willing volunteers.

Enormous crowds attended the opening of Ramsgate's Festival of Light in Nelson Crescent, 11 July 1951. Mayors from all parts of Kent and London were invited. The focal point was the Tidal Ball: a rocket signalled the start and the guest of honour, Miss Dinah Sheridan, switched on the lights. All of this was rounded off with a grand fireworks display and a festival ball which was held at the West Cliff Ballroom.

The Oddfellows' Hall is situated in the High Street and is used by many local organizations. This fine display of flowers was the culmination of the Ramsgate Horticultural Society's annual chrysanthemum show in 1966. The spectators seem quite awed by the exhibits.

Ramsgate Town First XI, 1906/07. The football team comprised Stevenson, Hawkes (captain), Vincent, Laming, March, Debling, A. Martin, Boulden, Henson, Brooks, Money, Larkin, Dixon and Stevenson. They appear to have won the Challenge Cup.

A group of sportsmen from the works team of D.C. Heard & Co., a well-known building and decorating firm of Southwood Road, Ramsgate, c. 1948. Mr Heard, in the centre of the back row, was also a borough councillor for the St Lawrence ward in the early 1950s. From left to right, back row: Alfred Burlinson, -?-, Douglas Casley Heard, Alfred Samuel, -?-. Middle row: Derek Harvey, Mick Taylor, Raymond Bell, Frederick Charles Bell Snr, Dennis Davie, Peter Heard, Horice Curtis. Front row: John Burlinson Snr, John Jarman, ? Nichols.

Eight

Transport

Marina Esplanade. *c.* 1950. This imposing horse and his handler, Mr Ollie Bing, were familiar figures on the beach and around the town. The borough stabling was on the north-east side of St Luke's Avenue, opposite the rear of the South Eastern Gas Board premises, where the gasometers now stand. Today the yard is used by Briganda's scrap metal merchants. In the background is part of Merrie England amusements, showing the slide which brought fun, pleasure and happy memories to many children and adults alike.

Nelson Crescent, *c*. 1908. West End Dairy's depot was at 30 Addington Street and the majority of their produce came from their own farm at Cleve Court, Minster. Here are three of their milk floats all with the firm's name displayed in a prominent position. In the mid-1940s the business changed hands and was taken over and became Sharp's Dairies Ltd.

West Cliff Road, *c*. 1910. Mr Frederick Wellard is proudly posing for this fine photograph of his horse-drawn West End Dairy float in front of Ramsgate General Hospital. Sadly today the hospital presents a different picture following its closure in April 1998. It is now boarded up and its future is uncertain.

Mr Joseph King, prospective Liberal candidate for the Thanet constituency in the general election of 1906, is seated in the car next to his driver outside the party's committee rooms at 98 High Street, Ramsgate. His Conservative opponent, Mr H.H. Marks, won the contest with a majority of 1,193 votes. In the background is the shop of Mr F. Price, fruiterer and florist.

On Wednesday 24 March 1915, a class 4-4-0 goods train, number 29, did not stop at the buffers at the Sands station. It was one of many occasions when locomotives overran the turntable. Mr Alexander W. Saunders of Gravesend can be seen standing with colleagues on top of the crashed train, bucket in hand, assisting in the removal of water from the tender's tank before the locomotive could be returned to the rails. The middle of the three posters on the right warns of 'further reductions in passenger services'. This was no doubt because of wartime pressure, but such a warning is still topical today!

An ambulance parked outside Ramsgate fire station, Effingham Street, 1915. As part of Thanet's contribution to the war effort, the money required for this vehicle being raised by public subscription. The general public was allowed to view it on Monday 11 October, before it was transported over the channel to France. There a Thanet man would have the responsibility of being its driver. After twenty months' active service it was unfortunately destroyed by shellfire on 24 April 1917.

This accident occurred on the corner of Grange Road and St Augustine's Road on Sunday 2 July 1919. Three visitors to Ramsgate, Mr and Mrs Hickman and their nine-year-old daughter, were seriously injured on their way to Sandwich. The army lorry of No. 1 Mobile A Battery from Herne Bay containing four soldiers was driven by Mr Frank Morrison, who was later charged with being drunk in charge of a motor vehicle.

Ramsgate railway station, c. 1950. The goods train and wagons are a sight seldom seen on our railway today. Steam has given way to electricity, but the thrill of the steam engine far surpasses that of today's electric or diesel engines.

Railway goods yard, 1930s. The main entrance to this complex is in Newington Road. This goods yard and the new Ramsgate and Dumpton stations were built and brought into use by 1926. They linked the South Eastern & Chatham Railway to the South Eastern Railway, doing away with the awkward terminal stations at Margate and Ramsgate.

Ramsgate's Royal Harbour, 1966. This adaptable Westland SRN6 hovercraft arrived in the harbour on Thursday 10 February. It was capable of carrying thirty-eight passengers or 3.1 tons of freight. The intention was to start a new cross-channel passenger service from Ramsgate to Calais. The hovercraft is in effect a ship that flies: it is capable of low-level flight over most types of terrain on a cushion of air formed by the action of downward directed fans. It is faster than most conventional ferries and is much quicker to load. November 1965 saw the formation of Hoverlloyd Ltd, the first company in the world to operate an international service.

Within two years Hoverlloyd Ltd had progressed to this larger SRN4 hovercraft, seen here at the new hoverport on the shore of Pegwell Bay. This craft was capable of carrying 200 passengers and thirty cars. The journey from Pegwell Bay to Calais lasted approximately forty minutes, and the vessel reached speeds of up to 60mph. Here a visiting group of students are observing this craft with admiration and awe.

Nine

Out of Town

Pegwell hamlet, c. 1750. This early print shows a very idyllic scene, with the hamlet nestling on the edge of cliffs overlooking a magnificent bay. The origin of the name Pegwell is unknown, but is has been suggested there is a connection with the springs which emerge from the cliffs. Many names have applied to this location, including Hopes Bay, Greystone Bay (1784) and Courtstairs. The latter is a reference to the Court Baron, held in ancient times at Nether Court. In 1837, Mr Cramp, the landlord of the Bellevue Tavern, served up such delicacies as potted shrimps and shrimp paste. Because Princess Victoria had visited the tavern with her mother, he was appointed 'Purveyor of Essence of Shrimps and Potted Shrimps in Ordinary to Her Majesty Queen Victoria'.

Pegwell village, c. 1863. The dominant building in this view is Tatnell's Clifton Tavern. Mr Tatnell, once the landlord of the Bellevue Tavern, moved across the road to these new premises, which had a small garden at the foot of the cliffs. This new venture catered for all, though primarily for the holiday trade. Many visitors arrived here in the popular horse-drawn brakes. This building became part of the Working Men's Club and convalescent home in 1898.

Pegwell village, c. 1907. This is a scene of enjoyment, with a number of visitors meandering around the village and an empty brake returning to Ramsgate, having dropped off its passengers. Bangers, famous for its potted shrimps, looks very busy. On the far right is the new annexe (built in 1906) to the Working Men's Club. The passageway connecting the two buildings runs through a tunnel under the road.

On 10 March 1947 a 100ft stretch of Pegwell Road in front of the Union Convalescent Home collapsed onto the beach below. This could have been a serious event but luckily no-one was caught in the collapse. The road was immediately closed and the East Kent buses were diverted along Down's Road.

The Working Men's Club and Union Convalescent Home are decked out in flags, bunting and photographs of Queen Elizabeth II to commemorate the Coronation in June 1953. This convalescent home was extended in 1898 to include the new Belvedere Tower. Mrs Passmore Edwards laid the foundation stone on Saturday 10 July 1897. The home prospered until the late 1960s but later became the Hovertel. With the closure of the Hoverport it was renamed The Pegwell Village Hotel. Because of the building of the new road to the Harbour and the need to tunnel underground, the hotel had to close. However, now that all the construction work is completed, we have seen a refurbishment of this fine landmark, now known as the Pegwell Bay Hotel.

Pegwell Bay, *c.* 1932, a photograph produced by local photographer Samuel Carr & Son of 36 High Street, Ramsgate. What wonderful holidays these campers must have had! Here they have the beauty of the bay, cliffs and – who knows – if they were interested enough they may have found a few fossils in the bay's sandy clay. Note the lone house on the Sandwich road.

An aerial view of Sandwich Road, *c.* 1957, encompassing the Danish ship *Hugin* with its great dragon figurehead, a replica of the type of vessel which once visited our shores 1,500 years ago. In the backgound is St Augustine's Hotel and Viking Ship Restaurant, which once included a fine dance floor. The hotel was demolished in January 1999. The green surrounding the Hugin is still an attraction for holidaymakers and locals alike and has become a popular picnic area.

Ramsgate International Hoverport, c. 1969. The Swedish-owned Hoverlloyd Company's reception building shown here greeted travellers on their arrival for an exciting form of travel from Thanet to the Continent. The fast documentation and customs clearance enabled Hoverlloyd to run up to twenty-eight crossings daily in peak seasons, each craft carrying 250 passengers and thirty cars.

After its initial trials at Ramsgate Harbour the hovercraft became a permanent feature of the town. Because of its growing popularity larger premises and craft were needed, so eventually a new hoverport was built at Pegwell which when completed was opened by Prince Philip in May 1969. Over the following decade market forces were not to the hovercraft's advantage and the Hoverport closed in October 1981.

Sandwich Road, *c*. 1902. In recent years there have been many changes in Cliffsend, but the Sportsman Inn is one building which has stood the test of time. Records of the inn go back as far as 1750. Three miles from Ramsgate, it was ideal for a trip out in one of the horse-drawn brakes and an excellent place to stop, especially for those on their way to Sandwich. Tomson & Wotton acquired the lease of this inn in 1872 and bought the freehold in 1927.

The Sportsman Inn was still a popular watering place in the 1930s, with its tea garden situated in a small wood next door. Later this area was used as a caravan park and more recently, permanent houses have appeared, adding to the village atmosphere.

Cliffsend post office and general stores on Foads Lane at the corner of Cottington Road, *c*. 1936. Note the contemporary transport on the right. The store has had a few alterations since: the entrance to the shop has been bricked up and a small window has been inserted. Part of the brick wall has been removed and an annexe has been built, which now houses the post office and store.

Cliffs End Lane, *c*. 1938, showing the wall behind which once stood the original Manor of Cliffsend. This was enlarged in 1876. Neither the manor nor the wall exists today. Where the brick wall stood is now a small green area. The cottage in the centre of this view was demolished for road improvements.

Cliffsend, *c.* 1930. These quaint, old-fashioned cottages dating back to 1737 are to be found in Foads Lane. This once sleepy hamlet has now been endowed with many new houses and bungalows, with the possibility of more in the future, dispelling once and for all the idea of a peaceful rural setting.

Foads Lane, Cliffsend, looking north, *c.* 1963. In times long past this place at the end of the cliffs was the preferred landing-point for many invaders, and many battles have been fought here. Today the battles are with the developers. However, this view has changed little in the last few decades.

St Augustine was the prior of a monastery in Rome when he was chosen by Pope Gregory to lead a band of forty monks on a missionary expedition to England. They landed at Ebbsfleet, on the Isle of Thanet, in AD 597 and were allowed by King Ethelbert of Kent to establish their headquarters at Canterbury. Here they built a monastery and Augustine became the first Archbishop of Canterbury.

Great Cliffsend Farm, with an abundance of lavender shrubs, c. 1955. It is a pleasure to cycle past during the late summer, to inhale the delightful aromatic fragrances of this very popular plant with its pale purple flower.

Manston village, *c*. 1905. The village played a notorious part in the Peasants' Revolt of 1381. The peasants' leaders, Wat Tyler and John Beecher, and 200 followers proceeded to Manston, entered Medmenham's house, ransacked it and burnt the rolls relating to the king's taxes. In more recent times, an air base and Royal Naval station were established here in 1916, contributing to the nation's survival through two world wars.

The Revd Canon T.G. Crosse MA, Rector of Ickham, conducted the dedication of this Manston war memorial on Tuesday 24 May 1921. He was formerly a vicar of this parish. The cross was unveiled by Colonel F.S. Cornwallis DL, JP, chairman of Kent County Council. The band of the Royal Air Force under Bandmaster E.J. Twitchett headed the procession and accompanied the hymns.

Grove Farm house, Manston, 1906. This farmhouse was built around 1820 in Georgian style. The front of the building is tastefully adorned with various creepers, suggesting a well-loved and lived-in dwelling. The farmland was sold to a development company in 1973 and in recent years quite a few new properties have been built, enlarging this once small hamlet.

Manston Grove Farm, 1907. These eighteenth-century barns were once used for the storage of farm vehicles and for the bedding of animals. The last occupants of Manston Grove Farm were Mr & Mrs N.H. Steed who lived there for twenty-two years. This particular postcard was originally sent to a Mrs Steer of Guildford Lawn, Ramsgate.

High Street, Minster, *c.* 1927, This unique fourteenth-century cottage can still be seen today; its outward appearance has little changed over the years. The village has always been a very popular venue for many visitors arriving by horse-drawn brakes and other modes of transport to explore this very interesting and historic area. In the past this cottage has been used as a guesthouse, tea-room and restaurant.

The interior of the Ye Olde Oak Cottage when it was a guesthouse, *c.* 1927. It is tastefully decorated to suit the atmosphere of its surroundings. The table is already neatly laid out awaiting the patrons of the day. Samuel Carr & Son of Ramsgate took both of these photographs.

120

Monkton, *c.* 1913. This splendid building, called The Croft, is still in existence today. However, the cottage on the extreme left and the beautiful trees have long since been removed. The Croft itself looks much the same today, and is reputed to date back to 1743.

Monkton, *c.* 1916. Monkton derives its name from the Monks of Christ Church, who were given this land by Queen Edgiva, mother of Edmund and Eadred, both kings in the year 961. This pleasant and tranquil scene, produced by Mr H.R. Farndon for the village post office, conveys us back to the year 1916. Just right of centre is the New Inn. The landlord in 1916 was Mr A.C. Hodgman.

A bustling scene outside the Red Lion Inn at Stonar, *c.* 1899. The landlord, Mr Walter Stratford, supplied accommodation and refreshments to the many travellers who came by this establishment on their way to and from the Thanet towns. Cobb and Co., the Margate brewery, has its sign prominently displayed on the front of the building. During its many years of existence a number of different brewers supplied this inn, the final one being Whitbread PLC of London.

Red Lion Inn, *c.* 1903. Opposite this inn there was once a thriving salt works, at a time when salt was a more valuable commodity than it is today. Note the humble dwellings to the right of the inn, probably the abodes of some of the salt pan workers at that time. Kelly's directory for 1903 lists the Red Lion Inn at Stonar as being occupied by Mr J.H. Chapman. Tomson and Wotton's sign can be seen on the front of the building. Unfortunately this landmark was closed in 1989 and after acquisition by Sandpiper South Ltd it was demolished in 1990.

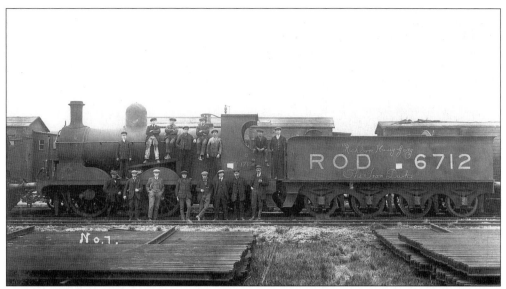

Richborough Port, known also as the Mystery Port, during the First World War. Here the 'heavy gang' proudly poses in front of the *Iron Duke* locomotive, ROD 6712. The port was connected by rail to Minster and conveyed gigantic amounts of military freight to the Western Front by ferry during the war. The photographer was C. Austen, of Southwood Road, Ramsgate.

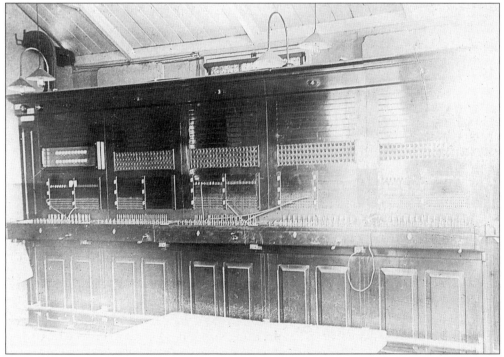

The switchboard at Richborough Port, 1920. The size of this telephone console indicates the immense area and complexity of the port. Around 20,000 people were employed in the port so good communications between the various departments was essential for the smooth running of day-to-day business.

Richborough Port, during the First World War. This is the interior of the machine shop, one of the finest to be found in the south of England. There were 106 tradesmen and sixty apprentices under the charge of Mr Pebbles, and fourteen labourers were responsible to Mr Gregory. The skills available here in this port workshop made it independent of most outside contractors.

Richborough Port was constructed by the Royal Engineers as an inland water transport repairs depot. Originally under canvas, the port grew to a city of huts and workshops. Shown here is one such shop with large wheel lathes. The workshops did every kind of repair work imaginable.

Richborough Port, 1916. A train ferry has finished loading and is about to start its journey to France. On arrival at port, these ferries could unload, load and be on their way in just under twenty minutes – scarcely different from modern ferries. Every type of war material imaginable was carried – including munitions, ambulances and tanks – but no passengers were carried. By 10 February 1918, 200,936 tons of material had been shipped out to Calais and Dunkirk and 59,922 tons had been received.

Train ferry No. 3, c. 1916. The general public knew little or nothing of the Mystery Port at Richborough. The port was the headquarters of the Inland Water Transport Company of the Royal Engineers, who controlled the supply of war materials to France. Train ferry No. 3 survived the First World War and, with the advent of the next war, she was once again taken over by the Royal Navy in 1939. She was converted in 1941 to a 'HSS' (Landing Ship Storm-Chute). She could carry 105 troops and either thirteen Mk I or nine Mk II mechanical landing craft. She was mined and sunk in March 1945.

An unknown group of Royal Engineers stationed at Richborough during the First World War pose near their superb quarters, 'Earwig Villa'. They are just a few of the thousands of men who assisted in the construction of this 1,500-acre port. Though this complex is called Richborough, the port site was at Stonar!

Richborough Port, c. 1919. With the cessation of hostilities the port settled into a steady decline. Depicted here is a monstrosity of a weapon captured by the British 4th Army; this along with other smaller items arrived at the port to be sorted and recycled by the women working here. Many were war widows trying to make a living for their families. One such lady was Jessie Florence Smith of Ramsgate, whose husband Thomas, of No. 4 platoon, 6th Service Battalion The Buffs, was killed in action on 13 October 1915.

Ten
Unidentified

It is with regret that I have not been able to establish or discover the where or who of these last few postcards. I hope that by publishing them someone will recognize them and enlighten us. If so, I look forward to hearing from you. This postcard shows a member of the Ramsgate borough fire brigade; the date is unknown, though probably sometime between 1915 and 1936. The location is at the rear of Ramsgate fire station in Effingham Street, but who is fireman No. 13?

This is a real disaster! On the back of this postcard there is a short written message: 'This is Ramsgate from James Street, where the water washed these houses down'. Was this person alluding to a deluge from a storm? You may note a number 18 displayed on the barrel to the left, I rather think it is the number of the photograph. Suggestions on this one would be very welcome.

Pegwell Road, c. 1948. This is obviously a very special occasion, with a superbly made cake in the shape of the Working Men's Club Union Convalescent Home. The people have defied all my efforts to identify them or the event, so I am asking for readers' help. Two of the men on the right could possibly be Mr R.S. Chapman and Mr W.E. Cornwall, the superintendents of the home.